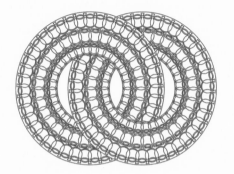

REWILDING

REWILDING

JANUARY GILL O'NEIL

CAVANKERRY
PRESS

CavanKerry Press Ltd.
Fort Lee, New Jersey
www.cavankerrypress.org

Publisher's Cataloging-In-Publication Data
(Prepared by The Donohue Group, Inc.)
Names: O'Neil, January Gill, 1969-.
Title: Rewilding / January Gill O'Neil.
Description: First edition. | Fort Lee, New Jersey : CavanKerry Press Ltd., 2018.
Identifiers: ISBN 9781933880686
Subjects: LCSH: Nature—Poetry. | Race—Poetry. | Family—Poetry.
Classification: LCC PS3615.N435 R49 2018 | DDC 811/.6—dc23

Cover artwork by Gray Jacobik
Book design and typesetting by Mayfly Design
First Edition 2018, Printed in the United States of America

CavanKerry Press is dedicated to springboarding the careers of previously unpublished, early, and mid-career poets by bringing to print two to three Emerging Voices annually. Manuscripts are selected from open submission; CavanKerry Press does not conduct competitions.

CavanKerry Press is grateful for the support it receives from the New Jersey State Council on the Arts.

ALSO BY JANUARY GILL O'NEIL

Underlife (2009)
Misery Islands (2014)

/ri'**wīld**/
verb
1. to reverse the process of domestication.
2. to return to a more wild or self-willed state.

(Rewild.com)

"Rewilding is one of those words a lot of people seemed to be waiting for. . . . I've plucked two out of the dozen or so definitions I've come across so far. One is the mass restoration of ecosystems, which means bringing back missing species. The other is the rewilding of our own lives—becoming enchanted once more with the natural world and letting go, for at least some parts of our lives, of that very ordered and controlled life we ordinarily lead."

—George Monbiot, author of *Feral: Rewilding the Land, the Sea, and Human Life*

CONTENTS

1

2

3

4

1

FAMILY PHOTO

You are sitting with our son
on the front porch, both in khaki shorts
and Superman T-shirts, faded blue and washed thin,
more casual than comic, the "S"
puffed out like shields on your chests.
The rhododendron next to you has overgrown
into a small tree, its spiraled leaves and pink flowers
cluster over the porch railing behind your heads.
It was 2006, our son soon to turn three
and our daughter, not in the picture,
would turn her first year, a year before
you started to turn from me,
from us. You are sporting a soul patch
because you knew I liked its scratch
against my skin. But I think even then
it was the root of something hidden,
a swirl of rot from the inside out.
The lines of your face show the edges
of what I thought was joy.
Even the potted plants beside you stood up,
wished us well on this tiny island of a porch,
not quite a fortress but a house full of solitudes
that grabbed hold of us, the absence of light
just beyond frame.

BRAVE

A thin layer of ash,
      fine debris, probably bone
            coated the windshield

as we passed exit after exit
      for the Garden State Parkway.
            We took detours and back roads

while police blocked every on-ramp.
      Blue lights pulsing.
            Officers in yellow hazard vests

stood next to their squad cars
      as we drove past midnight:
            my soon-to-be husband, mother-in-law

brother-in-law, and me
      in a 1992 Grand Marquis
            on our way to Virginia.

On the radio,
      nothing but news and static.
            All of us silent, sleepy, edgy,

uncertain, both absent and present
      on an empty highway
            driving past New York City.

———

I would never tell my daughter
      that some nights I lie awake
            listening for the raccoon I know is in the attic

but pretend isn't there.
       The scratching, the heavy scampering—
            she hears it, too.

If he were here,
       daddy would check things out.
            If he were here,

mommy would not feel lonely.
       We pretend to be brave,
            bang on the walls,

play loud music to scare it away,
       pray it does not have kits.
            Marriages fail.

There is no one else
       to go up there
            and get the little fucker.

————

On our day in court
       my lawyer was late,
            so the judge moved our case

to the afternoon docket.
       We sat for hours
            you on the left side,

me on the right
       listening to failure after failure,
            the quick dissolve of marriages into oblivion.

I remember thinking
       Hallmark doesn't make
            a card for this:

the moment when the judge calls your name
and uses words such as
irreconcilable, broken, and final

and a swell, no, a surge of tears
breaks as the judge
uncouples us.

You cried, too.
Neither of us looked at the other
or spoke.

When I turned around
You were gone.
You had left the building.

———————

Before we arrived at the hotel
We took engagement photos
in our wrinkled clothes.

And before that
we watched the sun rise as we crossed
the Chesapeake Bay Bridge Tunnel

And before that
we listened to Howard Stern around 5 a.m.
broadcast live, trying to find the right words. Any words.

And before that
you took the wheel from your brother
so he could get some sleep.

And before that,
silence.

And before that
	you held my hand
		as we rode in the back seat.

And before that
	we were not allowed
		on the Garden State Parkway.

And before that
	we stopped for gas, sandwiches,
		checked the check engine light somewhere in Connecticut.

And before that
	there was a toll
		on the Tobin Bridge.

And before that,
	I was on the phone
		with the maid of honor

who would ride the bus
	from Texas to Virginia to arrive by Saturday.
		I thought she was crazy.

And before that
	I was on the phone with my father
		who said, *be careful* and *I love you.*

And before that
	No flights were allowed
		out of Logan Airport or anywhere.

And before that,
	I said *yes.*

And before that
	You said *yes.*

And before that
      I asked, *Should we go through*
            with the wedding?

————

I would never tell my daughter
      male raccoons have no part
            in raising their young.

MUDLARKLING, DEAD HORSE BEACH

They're buried just past Winter Island
where the two-lane road winds
around the boardwalk at Salem Willows.
Dead Horse Beach, where the cold-blooded
flanks and loins of work horses
were discarded far from Salem Proper.
Here, the earth has taken them back
and given us silt. Why have I come here
at low tide, mudlarking
for bits of bottle and bone?
Even the renegade sky
has turned its back on every
gray cloud to be here.
It is the day before Mother's Day,
the kids with him for the weekend.
A breeze blows the new leaves
of the willow trees sideways,
their low-hanging branches lift and fall
against the wind, and on a hill just above
a family reunion, the backs of brightly colored
lawn chairs face me, I hear the occasional laugh,
smell the faint smell of grill.
Why have I come here today?
What am I looking for? I've come
to take off my shoes, to feel
blue and white shell fragments,
beautiful, broken mussels.
I've come to feel ache under my feet,
the deep ridges of shells
worn down by salt and time
while their insides are luminescence.
To hold one, midnight in my hands,

is to embrace what's been lost.
Fragments litter this beach—reeds,
shards of driftwood, whelks,
sea glass, a rusted chain, and this,
a gray anchor attached to a red rope.
Somewhere on the seam of sea
there's a small wish unbridled, adrift—

THE HURTING TIME

I come through the door
I've walked out of a hundred times
with a wordless wave

shrugging off the day's work
that rides on my shoulders, my bag
stuffed with ungraded papers.

Annie Lennox croons her sad song
like a long walk through low clouds.
To everything there is a purpose

she sings in large, breathy notes.
There's so much longing in the music
the cookbooks lean forward.

The kids helicopter around the kitchen
as I chop basil for tonight's dinner.
They go about the business of play

while I drift into the wake
of Annie's big, full voice.
I look outside to the backyard,

how her words get inside of me
like groundwater, heartache
after heartache. We know

memory is a passport that never expires.
I toss pasta into boiling water,
pick up the knife again,

let the lines of a poem fall out in neat rows.
I gather the choppings like lyrics.
That's when the hurting time begins.

KITCHEN FIRE

Soot turns cobwebs black.
It makes a white wall gray.
I wipe my finger along a surface
and it smears black as pitch,
my prints unmistakable—
the arsonist bathed in flame
or the pyro who loves her work.

The burnt smell stayed in the house
for weeks, seeped into boxes of flour
and pastas, slept in the curtains,
settled on glass, burrowed deep
in the pages of every book
on every shelf.

You might think me lucky
that the damage was minor—and if by lucky
you mean stupid, then yes,
I am lucky.

Even now
when I feel most safe,
while the children sleep
and I have no more names
to call myself, I look up at the ceiling
to find a single dark silk strand dangling,
thick as my daughters' hair. I close my eyes
and see the terrible billowing.

THE CROW

—For Maria Mazziotti Gillian

The Crow sits on my shoulder,
as I wait to enter the house of myself.
It guards the pit of my stomach,
the cave of the terrible truths
where all my secrets lie.

Not a kind word passes from beak to ear.
It spends its days scavenging for poems
picked down to the bone.
In its low, almost human voice,
it throws what I have not faced

back in my face, tells me I take more than I give,
that I'm a selfish daughter, a terrible mother,
even taunts me about the breakup of my marriage.
It says no one will believe I didn't see the signs—
the long hours my ex traveled for work

never happy to be back home,
how sex was as routine as mopping.
And when he left, how phrases like
"finding his authentic self" and "being in a good place"
became his new vocabulary.

The Crow, that trickster, murders language,
the thing I love most in the world—more than my own children—
reminds me that his girlfriend is not the first woman
he's cheated with, just the one he fell in love with,
the opposite of me, who protects and comforts him
in a way I can't possibly understand or fathom.

From Crow's mouth to God's ear.
Keeper of the cave, guardian of memory,
my Cerberus at the gates, the pit, the belly,
with eyes glistening. The one who stands at the edge
and says, *Enter at your own risk.*

TELL

Are you happy? Tell me what you're thinking. You blink when you speak. That's your tell. Everyone has a tell. Sitting in the red chair. In the corner of the family room which is not really a family room but a basement. The king sits in his basement throne. Red as a mouth. The whole room is a sham. It smells of the bleach I used to get mold spots off the wall. Behind the red chair. The wall looks as if I've taken an eraser to it. Tiny pencil points of mold remain. You've taken up smoking. You smell like an ashtray. That's your tell. I can tell. I'm losing weight. I can't eat. Hard time sleeping. Are you happy? I ask the obvious questions. That's my tell. I'm not happy. That's an understatement. We've only scrubbed the surface of my unhappiness. I'm sitting across from you sitting in the red chair, thinking how did we get here? Tell me how we got here. We walked down the stairs to the basement. Stop lying. It makes us look like fools. I don't want to be foolish. That's my tell. What about this new life of yours. Are you still with her? Tell me more about this authentic life you want to lead. I'm going to fumigate that red chair. Or burn it. If you were to die tomorrow, I'd show up at your funeral wearing a red microfiber dress. You're blinking again. What's left to say? I can see it in your pencil point eyes. King of the Basement. Tell me again what it means to live an authentic life.

A STAR CARESSES THE BREAST OF A NEGRESS (PAINTING POEM) JOAN MIRÓ, 1938

My breast is no longer mine. You have taken it
and made it a constellation
in your own negro sky.

You stand under the full moon
in a lonely room. I know you quiver when I pass.

Your life is alchemy and flat canvas.
Your life is curiosity and constant care.
Where is your ladder?

Well, I am not your escape.
I am a siren in a sea of stars and you are lost
in my corona. It is not a halo.
Each star is a wish that never came true.

2

SUNDAY

You are the start of the week
or the end of it, and according
to The Beatles you creep in
like a nun. You're the second
full day the kids have been
away with their father, the second
full day of an empty house.
Sunday, I've missed you. I've been
sitting in the backyard with a glass
of Pinot waiting for your arrival.
Did you know the first sweet 100s
are turning red in the garden,
but the lettuce has grown
too bitter to eat. I am looking
up at the bluest sky I have ever seen,
cerulean blue, a heaven sky
no one would believe I was under.
You are my witness. No day
is promised. You are absolution.
You are my unwritten to-do list,
my dishes in the sink, my brownie
breakfast, my braless day.

NIGHT AT THE ROLLER PALACE

After the birthday crowds thin out,
after the "Hokey Pokey" and "Chicken Dance,"
after the parents have towed their shaky kids
like cabooses ready to decouple
and the pint-sized skaters have circled the rink
like a gang of meerkats spun into a 10-car pileup,
you turn sideways and angle by as "Another One Bites the Dust"
thumps overhead. You give a finger point to the DJ stand
because, in your mind, we are soldiers in the march against time,
grooving to the retro beat while the disco ball shines overhead
cut crystal against rainbow walls.
You glide like Mercury or Apolo Ohno
without wings or skin suit, in low-rider jeans
that hug your body like you hug corners,
pass them all on the smoothed-out parquet floor,
worn down by time and rhythm. The trick is
to make it look effortless, remind them that
your quickness is a kind of love. You are the spark
between wood and wheel. And when your cranky kids
hang out by the wall ready to go,
holding those eight wheels by their brown leather tongues,
you give them a wave and keep circling,
Just one more song, you say.
This is your "me" time. It's all-skate.
You've got your whole self in—
That's what it's all about.

MAD LIB FOR ELLA

My Ella says the sky is the color of _snot_. If she could fit _pee_ and _poop_ into the conversation,
                                                       NOUN   NOUN

she would. My Ella is a proper noun. She's _fierce_. I watch her practice roundhouse kicks in _Tae Kwondo_.
                                  ADJECTIVE   SPORT

End of class, the instructor says, "give me _20_ sit-ups." Ella can only muster _one_ (she is her _mother's_
                                                    NUMBER   NUMBER   RELATIVE

daughter). The class cheers her on. Her _auburn_ curls tumble into her eyes like _Rotini_. Her laugh is boiling _pasta_.
                                          COLOR   FOOD   FOOD

We sit on the _bed_ playing Mad Libs. Snow falls like _spitballs_ from the sky; we bundle ourselves under
                  PLACE   NOUN

whispering sheets. Ella's feet are _cold_ as _calculators_. She says she has a _fire_-ache. I tell her I'm going to use that in
ADJECTIVE   ADJECTIVE   NOUN   COMPOUND NOUN

a _poem_. Says if I go outside, I should wear _fleece underwear_. When I tell her the three little pigs _happily_
 NOUN   ARTICLE OF CLOTHING   ADVERB

move to _Chicago_ to start a sausage business, she _giggles_ uncontrollably. Says one day, she wants to take the _gold_ medal
            CITY   VERB   COLOR

for _burping_ in the _naked_ Olympics.
VERB - ING   ADJECTIVE

HOPE YOU GET A PROMOTION TODAY

If you think I didn't,
you should stop reading now
because I did, but not the corporate-speak-
bottom-line-ROI-let's-look-at-the-numbers bullshit,
not the kind that involves the full weight
of a board or a committee or a panel,
where the news flies around the office like a hummingbird
and drowns in the water cooler, but the kind
that comes from your 11-year-old son
who says that exact phrase to you during
your morning goodbyes, before school,
in the kitchen with its stacked plates, bacon bits,
glops of waffle batter clinging to your robe
(which you call a *house coat* because it's a *coat*
for the house). *Hope You Get a Promotion Today*,
he repeats mischievously, flashing those baby browns
through his inch-long lashes—a phrase you're sure
he's heard but from where or from whom
is a mystery since you're not up for anything,
strapped to the tenure track, before the start
of classes and departmental meetings and
letters of wreck, certainly not Mom of the Year
or any conceivable writing award; perhaps
he says it because it's more interesting than
have a great day, see you later, love you,
or maybe it means all of those things in the same
odd manner in which you sit around the dinner table
asking your kids, *What did you fail at today?*,
and when they come back with nothing to say,
you look disappointed, for how else can you show them
how to try/risk/fail/endure, so for a brief moment
you forget you're in your bathrobe (house coat),

forget the ceiling with its peeling paint and see—
really see—your child who today said something brilliant,
risky, silly really, which is better than a promotion,
a promotion of the heart, if you will. You can honestly say,
Yes, sweetpea. I just did.

THE CATHEDRAL

—*After Rodin's* The Cathedral

I watch my daughter imitate
 the pose of Rodin's Cathedral.
  Her arms curved in slow gyration.

It is her way of understating
 the dark bronze, how two arms
  can captivate the imagination

in their dizzying swirl,
 find balance between
  light and shadows. In truth,

the hands are both right hands
 turning in on themselves, an architecture
  almost sacred, serpentine, yet protective

of the space within, of what the
 bronze cannot hold. My daughter bends
  uncomfortably away from me, resistant, as if

her whole body is questioning
 what it means to be a girl.
  She sees—maybe

for the first time—what is there
 and what is not from the hollow
  her hands make, all the empty angles

that never touch,
 the almost-grasp of the intimate.
  Her wrists slight and glistening

with summer's patina,
      her fingertips conjure her being
            and becoming,

body and soul
      closing and opening
            at the same time.

THE ROOKIE

America under the lights
at Harry Ball Field. A fog rolls in
as the flag crinkles and drapes

around a metal pole.
My son reaches into the sky
to pull down a game-ender,

a bomb caught in his leather mitt.
He gives the ball a flat squeeze
then tosses it in from the outfield,

tugs his cap over a tussle of hair
before joining the team—
all high-fives and handshakes

as the Major boys line up
at home plate. They are learning
how to be good sports,

their dugout cheers interrupted only
by sunflower seed shells spat
along the first baseline.

The coach prattles on
about the importance of stealing
bases and productive outs

while a teammate cracks a joke
about my son's 'fro, then says,
But you're not really black . . .

to which there's laughter,
to which he smiles but says nothing,
which says something about

what goes unsaid, what starts
with a harmless joke, routine
as a can of corn.

But this is Little League.
This is where he learns
how to field a position,

how to play a bloop in the gap—
that impossible space where
he'll always play defense.

HOODIE

A gray hoodie will not protect my son
from rain, from the New England cold.

I see the partial eclipse of his face
as his head sinks into the half-dark

and shades his eyes. Even in our
quiet suburb with its unlocked doors,

I fear for his safety—the darkest child
on our street in the empire of blocks.

Sometimes I don't know who he is anymore
traveling the back roads between boy and man.

He strides a deep stride, pounds a basketball
into wet pavement. Will he take his shot

or is he waiting for the open-mouthed
orange rim to take a chance on him? I sing

his name to the night, ask for safe passage
from this borrowed body into the next

and wonder who could mistake him
for anything but good.

GRACE

My dad used to call me
"Gracie" whenever
I was clumsy.
A spilled glass of water
or a trip down the stairs
earned his anger. He'd get
that stern look
on his face that said,
There she goes again.

When my daughter
drops guinea pig food,
small pellets on hardwood floor—
brain working faster than
her little hands can manage—
I look through her
with my father's eyes
not knowing who
will speak first.

SWEET'N LOW

Those little pink pillows of sweetness my mom
kept ziplocked in her purse for coffee on the go,
promising a taste just as good as sugar but not.

She kept them in the same pocket as cellophane-
wrapped peppermints and Juicy Fruit gum
to stave off my father's diabetic drops,

before the insulin stick, something pan-fried—
pork chops and gravy—as the greasy down-homeness
of Norfolk, Virginia rises above sea level.

That navy town, that model of a model U.N. town
where I grew up, those sweet tea days with a layer of
white grit lining the bottom of our lives. At age nine

I knew the difference between real and imitation, knew how
to navigate between dark and light, black, white, Filipino, Jewish.
Before Rodney King asked if we could all get along,

we did, at corner of Skyline and Redbook where the knockabout kids
would meet up for Hide and Seek, Dodge Ball, and Pickle,
where the parents watched out for each other's children,

planted in their lawn chairs, fly swatters in hand,
as we waited for the ice cream truck's ethereal music.
Bomb Pop or Push-Up? Nutty Buddy or Creamsicle?

35 cents could bring out a moment of sweetness
and there was nothing sweeter than watching
day vs. night. *Tag, you're it!*

Flashlight laser tag: brighter than lightning bugs,
more humid than hot, the scent of honeysuckle thick as Jean Naté
splashed under my arms to cover the summer stink,

before deodorant and leg-shaving, before boys became boyfriends,
when the heart could still repair itself from the outside in
when home was base, my dad calling my name

through the silver mesh of the screen door. Even now
at dinner out with my kids, I look for those pink packets
lodged between Splenda and sugar. I don't trust all happiness

and no calories. I always go for the real thing.

ON SEEING GWENDOLYN BROOKS AFTER HER READING AT LIU BROOKLYN, FEBRUARY 1996

What did we know about place?
What did we know about modesty and modest
fortunes, taking a table at Junior's
after hearing Gwendolyn Brooks read
her *Annie Allen* poems, after hearing "We Real Cool,"
with all of her soulful stress
on the "We."

We were college kids lurking late,
our first time across the bridge, ordering two slices
of cheesecake and four waters at this
round-the-corner place where the locals eat,
where the mayor visits and future presidents stop
on the campaign trail, our table center lit
by a single candle.

And in walks Ms. Brooks,
her small party clucking behind her,
hair wrapped in a black scarf—
she's the toughest nail in a roomful of hammers.
The waiter kneels to take her order,
brings over straws wrapped in white paper
and there she is, not being famous,
not being envied for all her sweet attention.

And here we are, tongue tied and dumb struck—
the lucky fools on Flatbush Avenue.
There must have been enough bravado
among us—although then I thought it was savvy—

to send a slice of pie over to her table.
Cherry. American. Red fruit dripping out of its flaky crust
and onto the bone-white dish.

She walks over to thank us for the kindness.
We respond with awkward smiles—
none of us with enough nouns or verbs
to make a sentence. Larger than life
standing at the edge of our table,
she lowers her ruddy, beautiful
moon face and asks if we want
a taste from her glorious plate.

MAYBE THE MILKY WAY

My son fills the inner space between my arm and body.
We lay in wet grass in the heart of the White Mountains,

far from the glare of city lights. *Maybe it's the Milky Way.*
Orion's belt drifts in a hemisphere so crowded with stars

we cannot locate it. We laugh, finger fine clusters of yellow-white
to create spirographs in star fields, our empty hands outstretched

and hungry—for what? We do not know. Like a private tour
of a planetarium's dome, it is our night. We know the stars

are watching us, would cast our shadows into the next galaxy
if they could. They watch him as I watch him, light reflecting light,

his beauty too dangerous to touch or hold or explain.
The love for my son would incinerate us if I get too close.

Tonight our hands girdle the heavens as we write new names
for ourselves, wishing on stars that neither shoot nor fall,

dissolve into stardust, while the campfire smolders
and the marshmallows, unattended, burn orange to black.

AT WOLF HOLLOW

Wolves do not howl at the moon.
They do not dream of walking upright
or seducing young girls in red hoods.

They were not put on this earth
to explain themselves to us
trapped in our claustrophobic flesh.

The stones they mark, the stubbled field,
the house that is their house
under the moon that is

their moon, illuminating thistle
and tree hearts rotting, the wind that imagines
silence and then delivers.

To think wolves howl at the moon
is lunacy: their chorus to the night
is a survival song.

And at the center of this pack
a single mother, alpha,
muscular and lean—

a savage grace at work
as she lifts her voice
to claim the dark.

3

FIRST SNOWFALL

Winter's arrived, that Johnny-come-lately.
The party starts tonight with heavy wet flakes
big as confetti, white clusters in
a snow spiral, always downward.
I feel like an outsider inside this space,
my burrow, my haunt, my home,
with the slush of plow scraping down
our lamplit street. The air feels decadent,
thick with want, while the commuter rail
whistles its long night-chord of passing.
The sky, a tabula rasa no one dares
to write upon, so what should I say
as the birches hold out their arms
like a good host, waving goodbye
to all the guests? Bundle up.
Here's the exit, your way out.
Here's the world with no one in it.
This is a party for one.

KETTLING

The low winter sun made driving difficult.
To look down the black asphalt
blurred my eyes. So for a few moments
I looked away, studying
the rock ridges and cliffs carved
out of cragged earth, the
marshy fields of phragmites
their silken heads standing swordlike
in the steady wind.

Above, a kettle of vultures
soared on the thermals, shadows
flying in upright spirals. You can't understand
in that moment how I yearned to be free,
free of the body and all its fog,
untouchable under the whisper of heaven,
rising and falling under my own power,
a current running in me and through me.
A whim of wind, a miracle.

I followed the span of wings
until I had seen enough, until
the long vine of highway
called me back to this world, said
keep going.

JANUARY THAW

Ducks circle the half-frozen pond
      in front of my children's school.
            They did not fly south for the winter

nor are they bothered by the stream
      of afternoon cars, the shuffle
            of backpacks and bodies.

They circle cumbersome ice chunks
      bobbing in and out of chilled water
            as they search for dragonfly eggs

and lacewing remnants
      preserved beyond
            their expiration dates

in the rooms
      made by pond weeds
            and small shafts of afternoon light.

At the curb there is the crush
      of kids hugging parents,
            The *how was your day*, and

Where did you sit at lunch
      and *let's go let's go let's go!*
            But in the center

a family floats, considers the soft wind
      traveling from shallow to deep and back again
            with no place else to be.

UNNAMING THE WORLD

My daughter says there's a signal for water.
I ask her what she means and of course
she's moved on to something else. She says this
under a sky the color of vellum—no water in sight.
We unname what we name, I guess.
        There is a noise, the color of living, like a cello.
When she plays, I dream of rocks being thrown
into a swollen sea. Her hands, twin starfish. Either way,
my heart skips like gray stones that kiss the surface and fly
before sinking.
        When we fly, we find our fire, she tells me.
Also, *the blue part of a flame is the hottest and hurts the most.*
That's why we're attracted to flames.

THINKING OF LUCILLE CLIFTON'S "IF I STAND IN MY WINDOW" AT THE CONVENT

—St. Marguerite's Retreat House

Who wouldn't want to lower her nightgown
or raise her blouse and push her breasts,
nipples tight as raisins, against the frosted window,
forming raindrops around dark clouds on a cold December morning.
No thing to bear witness except the 100-year-old pines
and a stray doe as it turns and scampers into the brush.

I think of the women here who married God,
to have and to hold no other, their black habits draping down
to the floor, and the young girls who stayed here
when the convent was an orphanage, the childhood of girls lived in wards,
learning to love each other like family with God as their father.
Did they peer out the window down to the lonely bench
and wish for the startle of a boy? A mother's call? Or a life beyond this?

A breast on glass is nothing but a marker of time.
Who wouldn't want to raise a blouse and announce to the world
I am here.

HOW A STAR DIES

Sometimes gravity wins. Sometimes stars burn bright
and hot but cool off quietly and beyond our reach.

Rooftops know this, as do empty neighborhood streets
and chill winds blowing through the barely open window.

Much of that light is wasted, yet it illuminates this house,
this bed in which I sleep alone. Without the darkness

I would have never seen it. Everything is finite,
even love. It sputters and fades like a white dwarf,

a cooling ember that on a clear night
would be overlooked for some other beauty—

a scattering of stars whose light keeps coming
in waves. The grace-ache of killing time.

LOVE SONG FOR THE
DECOMMISSIONED POWER PLANT

After the workers clocked out,
  after the financiers and analysts,
   after the risk assessors,

after the mayor, the developers, the hazmat teams,
  the environmentalists, reporters, and electricians
   after the demolition crew and hazmat teams

(again), the VCs and architects,
  the bankers and the 1-800-Junkers,
   they sent in the artists

to reimagine the destruction—the photographers
  who captured particlized air in a shutter,
   fog rising inside the building,

dank and chilled and unforgiving.
  What does ghost-hollow feel like?
   Ask the sculptors

who will configure boxes upon boxes of steel rods,
  fissures, and orange wire connectors into something astonishing.
   What happens to all that sacrificed zinc, the cheapest of metals,

the last vestiges of the industrial age?
  Ask the playwright, who will recreate stripped copper
   and brass as backdrop to his next dystopian production.

Who will speak for the cinder blocks
  and silent machinery? Who sees
   gray turbines grand as whales surfacing?

After the cranes and dumpsters leave,
    who will foretell the coming of green space
        pushing up through the seepage of mud

as if the world has already happened?
    Ask the poets, who will write this new space into being,
        the sky tilting a little closer to the sun

glistening over the gray waters of the Atlantic.
    They are trained to harness power
        where there is none.

SOBER

Today I saw a motorcycle
>with a license place that read
>>SOBER above its back fender.

I've seen it here before, parked
>along the scaffold-covered sidewalk
>>next to the old campus library

set for demolition.
>Whose is it, I wonder.
>>Which student, which teacher

enters the morning
>half lost in shadows to park
>>next to ruin every day?

I can stand for hours watching men
>in red hard hats, etched in tattoos,
>>spraying down rubble with water hoses

to keep dust from flying
>into the blue September sky
>>while another wall falls,

watching an excavator stretch
>its giraffe neck to remove concrete
>>and steel from the cadaverous body

now hollow, long drained of life, unstable
>under the weight of words, under
>>the knowledge of itself.

How easy it is to get caught up
>in destruction, and how hard it is
>>to rebuild

back from obliteration—
>   not from one massive implosion
>   or the forged steel of a wrecking ball,

but drawing the earth backwards piece by piece.
>   Maybe the bike belongs to a hard hat
>   who wears ruin like a safety vest,

like scaffolding
>   coiled in the greenest ivy
>   as the process of rewilding begins.

4

OLD SOUTH MEETING HOUSE

We draw breath from brick
    step on stones, weather-worn,
        cobbled and carved

with the story of this church,
    this meeting house,
        where Ben Franklin was baptized

and Phillis Wheatley prayed—a mouth-house
    where colonists gathered
        to plot against the crown.

This structure, with elegant curves
    and round-topped windows, was the heart
        of Boston, *the body of the people,*

survived occupation for preservation,
    foregoing decoration
        for conversation.

Let us gather in the box pews
    once numbered and rented
        by generations of families

held together like ribs
    in the body politic. Let us gaze upon
        the upper galleries to the free seats

where the poor and the town slaves
    listened and waited and pondered
        and prayed

for revolution.
    Let us testify to the plight
        of the well-meaning at the pulpit

with its sounding board high above,
        congregations raising heads and hands to the sky.
            We, the people—the tourists

and townies—one nation under
        this vaulted roof, exalted voices
            speaking poetry out loud,

in praise and dissent.
        We draw breath from brick. Ignite the fire in us.
        Speak to us:

the language is hope.

ON BEING TOLD I LOOK LIKE FLOTUS, NEW YEAR'S EVE PARTY 2014

Deep in my biceps I know it's a compliment, just as
I know this is an all-black-people-look-alike moment.
So I use the minimal amount of muscles to crack a smile.
All night he catches sight of me, or someone like me, standing
next to deconstructed cannoli and empty bottles of Prosecco.
And in that moment, I understand how little right any of us have
to be whoever we are—the constant tension
of making our way in this world on hope and change.
You're working your muscles to the point of failure,
Michelle Obama once said about her workout regimen,
but she knows we wear our history in our darkness, in our patience.
A compliment is a complement—this I know, just as the clock
will always strike midnight and history repeats. This is how
I can wake up the next morning and love the world again.

TOM BRADY'S BALLS

*"To me they're perfect. I don't want anyone touching the balls . . .
I don't want anyone rubbing them."*

—TOM BRADY

Look at him, muscular
and kind of knowing
with his shoulders loose,
with his boy face and blue eyes,
tussle of hair under his helmet,
the way he squeezes the ball
and you say, oh hell yeah,
game on. So it begins,
the drop back, catch
and release, leather
not tacky or thin or altogether
round, yet somehow perfect
in the palm, loosening up
in his warm hands
giving into the cool open air.
Quiet the chatter. Say turf
and fire. Set and spark.
Throw it—nothing fancy,
just a perfect spiral,
high and tight,
mass into energy
powering the universe.
Watch it rise and fall,
dropping into the promise
of our lives. Goodnight,
Irene. Fuck yeah,
he's got balls.

TINDER

Admit it: you miss the sex.
That part of you closed up shop,
hung a *Gone Fishing* sign
on the marriage after it ended.

It is an unattended campfire
burning itself to the embers
on a cold January night, bits of ash
floating into the air and disappearing.

How can you not think of the campers
around the fire ring, leaning in to warm
their hands over hot tinder? Small kindling
laid over tops of logs. Like a survivalist
you have learned to live on less.

It burns from the inside out
from a place you had forgotten,
where the hot coals reveal what you really are:
awake, ablaze, afraid, alone. A good camper
never leaves a campfire unattended.

You know you are more like the alders
bordering the encampment,
more like a twig among the thin,
brittle branches of leafless trees,

more like the pleasure of the tongue,
the lift and compression of breasts held
closer to the glowing red heart,
closer and closer to earth and below
to the in-door turned out-door
after baby after baby. Oh, baby—
anything can be ignited by a match.

ODE TO NO

Beautiful N word.
A one-word sentence.
The whole note of finality.
The last stand. The absolute.
The sacred negation of desire.
Simplicity. Not another word
produces such dejection.
Like the color black it absorbs
light. Colorless, odorless,
at times tasteless—full of lack,
of what's not needed. Sometimes
it's exactly what I need.
Refusal of all passage; access denied
into the country of want.
Can a single word
save me from myself?
It is the humblest of speeches.
A blank page. An unopenable door.
What is more inviting than the word no?
In the war of desire it is the smallest weapon,
the sharpest spear. I want what you have.
The answer is no.

THE NIGHT I WORE THE PURPLE DRESS

I was Chambord floating
in bubbles of Prosecco. I was
a scallop wrapped in bacon.
Sleeveless, with seams that contoured
and material that breathed,
I liked when men placed
the flat of their hands
against my back
against the gold zipper running
down the length of my dress.
Easy access, I teased.
This dress with the zipper
like the Mississippi flowing
the entire length of the United States
meandered toward the Gulf of Mexico
down in the Delta.
It owned me, that dress,
dark as night but not night
dark as closed eyelids,
the wispy, veiny, purplish light
that seeps through when making a wish—
a condition of longing
that creates more longing.
Was I indigo?
Was I amethyst or cobalt?
That night I was the life
of the party, in a dress
the color I could not name.

FIRST SEX AFTER DIVORCE

I'm eating an Empire
after cursing the tree.
The crunch. The tear. The juice
streaming from the corners
when there's too much
in the mouth. Where to put
the tongue, and how to make
it last. The tart perfume.
The beautiful stem. The small seeds.
Freeing the peel from the skin
and the dissolve into pulp.
The next bite. Then the next.
Eve knew what she wanted
long before it had a name.
The curved structure.
The mounded flesh. A grove
within a grove. An orchard
red and hot. Praise the tree
from which it fell and the gravity
that brought it down. Praise what remains.
Praise Newton's Third Law of Motion.
Praise the physics of cupping my hands
around the fruit. Praise the fruit itself.
Praise the doctors who prescribe it daily.
Praise hunger. Praise sweet want.
The feast of flesh and the hard cider.

CONFESSION

On this night we tried to repair each other,
replace the parts stolen by our ghosts.

Outside, the rain is unrelenting but inside
I open in his strong hands, my unfolding

his folding, a Möbius strip of grievance
and grief. In the cathedral our bodies make

we worship each other in tongues.
We shimmer in sweat. We come

apart at the seams. In the dark
we are neither angels nor shadows.

Unrepentant, down on our knees,
we rise and rise and rise.

ALCHEMY

"Out beyond ideas of wrongdoing and rightdoing,
there is a field. I will meet you there."

—Rumi

—*For Jennifer Jean*

Love, I'm expecting you
to walk through the door

in a suit and sneakers. Belly up
to the bar and order me a sidecar

or a blueberry mojito.
You know me so well, Love,

I'm sitting at the bar's reverse curve,
the stools are worn leather,

the wood's polished smooth.
I'm feeling lacquered and varnished,

Love. I am dark with possibility.
I'm looking for the remix on the B side

of the collector's edition and that's rare,
Love, I dream an alchemy that rounds

the mouth into a kiss and makes it last.
Love, I hear crickets chirping in a field

of wildflowers and have mistaken them for you.
We are social insects in this hot-spot buzz-kill,

on this pheromone trail of tears
yet I'm attracted to your song.

Love, I am smiling with my eyes. Love,
I have hitched my hopes to the wrong stars

in bars, I have muddled
the waters with ice and mint

but there is no substitute for pleasure,
which is all mine, which is all right.

Love, I'm adorable.
Love, I come with a twist

of lime off the rim of the glass.
What are you having, Love?

You are here and it is now.
He loves me, he loves me not.

Love, pull the petals off that flower.
My arms are a bouquet of broken stems.

HUGGING THE CELLO

This morning I watched my daughter
unpack her new cello out of its black
vinyl bag, cherry wood, lacquered
a rough sheen gleaming
from its wide bout.

I have seen this face before—stern,
determined—all business as she wraps
her small fingers around its neck,
the scroll resting on her shoulder
the outline of a body on a body,

from the navel to where
the bridge begins, its ribs
sloped against her ribs,
the middle curve a snug fit
between her knees

while she draws back the horsehair bow
pulling the strings into a sound
deep as a groan, almost voice,
fingers moving without
form or technique,

the truth of her body leaning into the music.
Already she knows how to shape
a sort of song, which comes
as easy to her
as breathing.

HERE, NOW

A black and white caterpillar
climbs a tall blade of grass
among patches of wild thyme.

Further down the gravely path
a butterfly—maybe a monarch—flutters,
no, leaps ahead of me as soon
as I approach, then disappears
into a field of blooming milkweed.

Feathery white flowers sway
in the breeze, their silken seeds
taken by a slight gust of wind.

Here, now
on this ridge breathing mountaintop air,
I see what I have nearly crushed,
nearly missed.

UMBRELLA

Last night, I saw a long, blue umbrella
hanging on a table by its crooked handle.
A green and brown strap held
its collapsed ribs in place.
Whose is it? No one in sight.
Umbrellas carry their own currency
passed from friend to friend,
a spare on a car's back seat
waiting to be used. Umbrella,
from the word *umbra*, meaning shadow.
Not a parasol or bumbershoot
but something large, waterproof, telescopic,
stretched wide, spun on its tip
by my daughter in August rain.
Gene Kelly kisses Debbie Reynolds
under a black dome before he tosses it
and begins to sing, and Rhianna twirls,
splashes puddles, asking us to stand under hers.
Does anyone ever buy an umbrella?
Maybe before or during a downpour
but never after. I have seen too many
left behind in frustration, poking out
of trash cans, their spikes pointing skyward,
or flipped inside out by a harsh wind. Or worse—
forgotten in movie theaters or subway cars.
No, there is grace in a left-behind umbrella
picked up by someone who needs it more
at that particular moment, maybe when their sky is falling
or caught by surprise. Once, at dinner
with my best friend at a Chinese restaurant,
we're the last ones in the place,
nothing but broken fortunes and the check

in front of us. *How will we make it as writers?*
we asked each other. Then the sky opened
up, heavy drops for blocks and blocks.
There in the corner a black umbrella
leaned against the glass doors, waiting.
As we paid the check, the man behind the counter
said *take it.*

AT MILLAY COLONY

Close
door gently!
Another baby
bird fell
from the nest.

read the note
stuck to the glass door
with Band-Aids.

Tiny tufts of down, soft
as cotton, caught
in the doormat's fibers.

And above: the nest
made from snips of grass,
twigs, moss, resting

between floodlights
under a wooden awning.
Warm at night. Safe

yet not safe. Every entrance
and exit a precarious journey.
Temporary roost.

For all her planning,
the mother's nowhere in sight.
Maybe she did not count

on the door's heavy slamming
when she hatched her clutch
or maybe she did,

knowing those fledglings
will follow her, beg for food
even after first flight.

When will they ever learn?,
she must have thought
her first summer afternoon away

flitting from branch to branch
looking for just the right spot
to sing her own complex song.

How it must have sounded—
cadenced, piercing—as if
she were hearing it for the first time.

NOTES

Rewilding quote ("Rewilding is one of those words a lot of people seemed to be waiting for . . .") by George Monbiot was first published online in the article "Rewilding the Land Can Repair Damage We've Caused and Reconnect Us to the Natural World" by Simon Worrall for *National Geographic*, October 10, 2014. http://news.nationalgeographic.com/news/2014/10/141008-rewilding-nature-george-monbiot-beavers-highland-clearances-ngbooktalk/

"On Being Told I Look like FLOTUS, New Year's Eve Party 2014": The phrase, "all-black-people-look-alike moment" is similar to a phrase in Claudia Rankine's book *Citizen* ("all black people look the same," pg. 7).

"Unnaming the World": The line "There is a noise, the color of living, like a cello" comes from a poem by Sean Thomas Dougherty.

ACKNOWLEDGMENTS

My deepest gratitude to the following publishers and organizations:

American Poetry Review: "At Wolf Hollow" and "Tell"
Green Mountains Review, Poets.org: "Hoodie"
Harvard Review: "Thinking of Lucille Clifton's 'if i stand in my window' at the Convent"
New England Review: "Brave" and "Mudlarking, Dead Horse Beach"
Paterson Literary Review: "Family Photo" and "The Crow"
Poets.org: "Old South Meeting House" and "On Being Told I Look like FLOTUS, New Year's Eve Party 2014"
PoetsArtists: "Tinder" and "Alchemy"
Prairie Schooner, Poets.org: "The Rookie"
Rattle, American Life in Poetry: "Sunday"
Sou'wester: "Night at the Roller Palace"
Solstice: A Magazine of Diverse Voices: "Sober"
Tab: The Journal of Poetry and Poetics: "Mad Lib for Ella"

Love to my sweetpeas, Alex and Ella. We miss you, Tim.

To my poetry peeps: Joseph Legaspi, Colleen Michaels, J.D. Scrimgeour, Danielle Jones-Pruett, Kevin Carey, Cindy Veach, Dawn Pawl, Jennifer Jean, Jennifer Martelli, Elizabeth Horowitz, Michael Ansara, Afaa Michael Weaver, Martha Collins, Susan Rich, Kelli Russell Agodon, Oliver de la Paz, and the community of poets and writers who make the everyday extraordinary. Thank you.

Special thanks to Mass Poetry and CavanKerry Press for their support.

CAVANKERRY'S MISSION

CavanKerry Press is committed to expanding the reach of poetry to a general readership by publishing poets whose works explore the emotional and psychological landscapes of everyday life.

OTHER BOOKS IN THE EMERGING VOICES SERIES

Rewilding has been set in Adobe Jenson Pro, an old-style serif typeface designed by Adobe's chief type designer Robert Slimbach in 1996. It is based on a text face cut by Nicolas Jenson in Venice around 1470.